I0472011

The Case to Fire Obama

with the November election

by Steven R. Jefferson

Table of Contents

Chapter One

Obama is failing; and he plans to fail more

I am going to explain for you how President Obama is failing, how he is hurting the country, and why that is exactly what he intended to do, and why he plans on doing it even more in his second term if he is re-elected! I know that this sounds outrageous. And I am not the first person to say it. However, it is relatively easy to illustrate with facts and logic. This little book won't take long to read, and it is easy to understand, so please, read on.

To get us started, and to help to give you a little perspective on the job of the President of the United States, let's do a little role playing exercise. In this little exercise you are the Chairman of the Board of a large corporation. The corporation is owned by many shareholders. You as the Chairman of the Board report to the Board of Directors. Your Board has assigned you the very important job of selecting and hiring an experienced executive to serve as the corporation's Chief Executive Officer. The CEO is an extremely important position. The CEO is the highest ranking corporate officer. The CEO is responsible for developing and implementing the high level business strategies that determine the corporation's direction for developing and selling its products and/or services, so that you can make money! The CEO makes decisions regarding capital investments, the use of business capital and debt financing to fund operations and investment activities, and the level of risk to be incurred or taken by the corporation in implementing business decisions and strategies. To simplify this some, the decisions that the CEO makes will determine the success or failure of the corporation.

So now let's continue your story as the Chairman. You interview a number of qualified candidates, and then you narrow the list down to the top two guys. Then you bring back these top two guys for another interview so that you can make your decision of which guy is the best one for the job. You ask them a lot of questions, and you carefully listen to the answers that they give you. How well can they communicate with, and inspire your employees to work hard and do their best? How well do they understand your industry, and your market segment, and your competition? Can they make the hard decisions or are they scared of making a mistake? (sometimes making no decision can be as bad as making the wrong decision) Are they being sincere and genuine with you, or are they telling you what they think that you want to hear? Do they have a vision for where they want to take your business for greater success, on day one on the job? These are some of the critical questions that you need to answer in order to make a good decision on who should be your CEO.

Well now you have completed the interview process. You spend some time evaluating the answers and the comments that the candidates gave you. You make a decision on which guy that you think can do the best job for the corporation. Now you hire the guy and you make him your new CEO. Then you get out of his way and you let him do his job as the CEO running the corporation.

Now let's fast forward three years and see how the CEO that you hired is doing, because as the Chairman it is your job to evaluate the performance of the CEO and the corporation, and to give feedback to your board of directors, and to make recommendations to the board based upon the performance and the resulting success or failure. Three years in to the CEO's tenure the corporation is not performing very well financially. The corporation's revenue actually declined in the first year, and then revenue grew only slightly in years two and three, clearly at a very disappointing rate of growth. The revenue growth rate is insufficient to improve the corporation's profitability. Because the corporation's income is not growing, and the profitability has declined, the corporation has had to lay-off some of the employees, because there is not enough work, and there is not enough cash available from operations to pay the payroll.

The CEO had some really big ideas about new products and how to grow the corporation's business. In order to produce these new products the corporation had to borrow a significant amount of additional debt for equipment and supplies and materials inventory. So the corporation's total debt has increased while the much needed revenue has not increased, and the profitability has completely disappeared. Now your corporation has become unprofitable, has a negative cash flow situation, and has more debt to repay than ever before. As the chairman of the board, you have a big problem and the responsibility to fix this big problem. What do you do? Do you give the CEO more time with the same ideas and strategies that have not worked? If the CEO has some new and different ideas and a willingness to make strategic changes, then you might consider giving him another chance. However if you know that he does not have any new ideas, and is unwilling to change his way of thinking, then you would be a fool to keep pursuing the same strategies that have resulted in such bad results. Repeating the same actions that bring bad results, and expecting a different outcome is defined as "insanity". So as the Chairman of the Board it is your duty to the corporation to fire this CEO and replace him with a better candidate, who has a new and different vision for how to run your business.

The role playing exercise that we just completed is a representation of the performance of the current President of the United States of America, Barack Obama. A necessary majority of the voters in November 2008 hired (elected) Barack Obama to be the Chief Executive Officer of the Government of the United States of America. Just like our corporate CEO in the story above, the U.S. President is supposed to formulate and implement policies that determine how the federal government will manage the nation's business. And preferably the results of the policies will produce success and growth in the economy and security for the nation. The President takes an oath of office to preserve, protect and defend the Constitution of the United States. It is incumbent upon the President in light of the oath of office, that his policies must also protect the interests of the United States, including the well-being of its citizens and the nation's economic health.

It is at this point that some people will say, hey you are just a partisan Republican so of course you are going to blame a democrat President for things that you don't like or that you disagree with. So let's talk about that. Just as the corporation and its CEO above had certain performance factors to evaluate, so too does the outcome of the policies of the President. So rather than talk about Barack Obama personally, or whether I agree or disagree with his political views, I will focus on the results that have been produced by his policies since he has been in office. Results are factual and not based on opinion.

Now as I begin to discuss the President's performance let me remind you that for his first two years in office, this democrat President's party held a majority in both the House and the Senate. This should have made it relatively easy for him to get his legislation passed by the Congress. As such he is responsible for the policies that were enacted. The first performance indicator that I will evaluate is the Gross Domestic Product ("GDP"). The GDP is one of the primary indicators of the health of the nation's economy. The GDP is the total dollar value of all goods and services produced in the United States. Another way of defining GDP is the "size of the economy". The most meaningful way to evaluate the GDP is by comparing it year to year, or quarter to quarter. This tells you if the economy is growing and by how much. If the GDP is either flat or negative, that is a bad indicator. If the GDP is growing slower than the rate of inflation, that is also a bad indicator. 2009 was this President's first full year. At the end of 2009 the national GDP (adjusted for inflation) grew by one-half of one percent. That is to say that the economy was flat in 2009. There was no growth. For some perspective, the average annual rate of growth of the GDP from 1948 through 2011 was 3.23%. Now we will kind of give this rookie President a little "pass" for 2009, given that the housing bubble had burst in 2008, and there was the banking and Wall Street crisis in 2008 as well. Plus he needs a year to implement his financial policies. So 2009 was bad, but not his fault. Now let's look at 2010. In 2010 the GDP grew by 3.14%, which is a good improvement over 2009. Maybe his policies are working and 2011 will get back above the average growth rate of the prior six decades, right? Not so much! In 2011 the GDP grew by only 1.6%. This is a very low rate of growth and far below the historical average. This is a bad indicator for the President's policy performance.

Now the President is two years in to his administration. Two years with full control of the House and the Senate, and the third year of his policies result in a GDP growth rate of only 1.6%. Folks that is not good. This is the United States of America. This is the largest and most dynamic economy in the world. When your policies are fully implemented and the results are GDP growing 1.6%, then there is something wrong. This is what I meant when I said this President's performance was on par with the failing corporate CEO in the little introductory story. And 2012 looks no better. The first quarter indicators are projecting the 2012 GDP will grow at about 2.0%. This is not even at the rate of inflation, which is running between 2 and 3 percent. This President's economic policies are not succeeding in growing the world's most dynamic economy. This will have significant consequences economically, socially and politically. It must get fixed immediately. Obama has no policy changes or adjustments to do so!

The second performance indicator that we will look at is the unemployment rate. For some perspective, the average U.S. unemployment rate from 1948 through 2011 was 5.7%. It has been widely agreed by economists that in the U.S. economy a 5% unemployment rate is considered to be relative "full employment". So if you are the President, that is a good goal to aim for. The unemployment rate in the U.S. at the end of 2008 when Obama was elected was 7.3%. It had started 2008 at 5.0% and was gradually increasing in 2008 as some extraordinarily bad economic events were taking their toll. In 2009 the unemployment rate grew to 10.0% in October and ended the year at 9.9%. Again we will kind of give the rookie President a "pass" for the 2009 unemployment rate given the events of 2008, and to give him a year to implement his policies to change the negative trend and make improvement. So, let's take a look at 2010. In 2010 the unemployment rate varied between 9.9% and 9.5% throughout the year and ended the year at 9.4%. That is not much improvement given that the President again had control of the Congress throughout 2009 and 2010, and he implemented some very expensive (federal spending) big-government oriented "pro-employment" programs that he promised would bring the unemployment rate down under 8.0%. Obviously the President's big-spending government oriented programs did not work. Remember the term "shovel ready" stimulus projects? Yea, right. The Stimulus program that was implemented by the Obama administration to improve the unemployment rate, cost the U.S. tax payers $825 Billion. That's not a misprint. That is Billion with a capital B! That is nearly one trillion dollars in one program. One failed program. It was 25% of the total federal spending in 2009! That was a very expensive "miss". Most of that money did not go toward job creation. A majority of the spending was used to prop up unproductive state and local level government jobs, and some was strategically funneled to unions and campaign funds that would later benefit the President and his party.

In fairness we should look at the unemployment rate in 2011. The unemployment rate remained above 9% through the first three quarters and ended 2011 at 8.5%. In the first quarter of 2012 the unemployment rate dropped to 8.2%. Well, you might say, maybe the President's policies are starting to work. Slower than we wanted, but the unemployment rate is declining, right? Yes, by the standard statistical calculations that would appear to be true. However a closer look at what is really going on will tell quite a different story. And this is one of the reasons that I got pissed-off and decided to write this little rant! You see, the "main stream media" does not tell you the whole story. So the average person on the street that will be voting in November needs to know the whole story! So here it comes…

The current unemployment rate is deceptive and inaccurate for two reasons. First, there is a large number of people who are unemployed and have been unsuccessful in finding suitable employment, so they have stopped looking for a job. Because they are not still seeking employment, they are not counted in the unemployed ranks by the government unemployment rate calculation. Second, there are a large number of people who do not have the luxury of not having a job. So instead of no longer looking for a job, they take a job that is below their qualification level and of course they are working for less money than they are accustomed to earning, based on their qualifications. So while the unemployment rate is being reported by the federal government as 8.2%, if you factor in the discouraged adults, and others working part time for lack of full-time employment, the unemployment rate is closer to 14%! (The U6 unemployment measure) If you add in the college graduates seeking their first job who are still in low skill positions, such as counter-work at

Starbucks (et al), then the unemployment rate is likely closer to 16%! Now those are shocking numbers. That means there are a lot of your fellow Americans who by no wrong doing of their own, are living less than the life they deserve because their President and their federal government are not doing the right things for this country.

Now I have given you two examples of poor performance by the President, and I have a third, which I will discuss next. You may be thinking, hey you are being unfair. You have not said what Obama should be doing instead of what he has done. Just wait, I will get to that. You see, there are different strategies that he could have used, and history indicates that the outcome would have been different. So yes, I will get to what he should have done, later in the book.

OK, the third performance indicator is the President's management of the national debt. This is where the story gets really bad. And honestly it is a little complicated. The debt issue is not 100% the President's fault. The Congress bears some blame as well. However, and this is the key, it is the

President's responsibility to either fix the problem or submit a reasonable plan for addressing it. Remember the President is the CEO of the country. He has to be the leader. This President has not given the Congress the proper leadership. Much like our wayward corporate CEO in the opening story, this President is pursuing his chosen ideologically driven policies without any regard for the long term consequences of his actions, despite the very obvious and negative results in the daily news headlines. The national debt has increased more during President Obama's three years in office ($4.9 trillion) than it did in eight years under President George W. Bush ($4.8 trillion). This is unsustainable debt growth. If you observe what is happening in western Europe to country's like Greece, Spain, Ireland and Portugal, as well as the trends in Italy, France and the UK, you will see what eventually will happen to the United States if our debt is not brought under control.

The most troubling aspect of Obama's mismanagement of the debt is that he never seriously discusses it and he has no plan or any apparent intention to deal with it. He appears to have no willingness to deal with it at all. Controlling the nation's debt growth is not a matter of great importance

to President Obama, if you view his policies and future plans for further

legislation. Everything that President Obama considers to be a priority

actually makes the debt growth crisis even worse! I will give you some

examples. First, in Obama's first year in 2009, when he announced his

plan to stimulate the economy, which was called "The Stimulus ", it was not

tax incentives that have been used successfully many times in our history.

His stimulus was a federal spending plan that adds to the annual budget

deficit and the total national debt. Government spending does not create

jobs or incentivize economic growth. It never has. If that worked, western

Europe would not be in the economic crisis that it is in now. And if

government spending worked, then the GDP and the unemployment rate

would have shown significant improvement in 2010 and 2011, which did not

happen! And it won't with Obama's policies! The second example of an

Obama legislation priority that has no regard for the growth of the national

debt is his signature bill passed by Congress and signed in to law in 2010,

The Affordable Healthcare for America Act, commonly known as

"Obamacare". We can argue the merits of that legislation separately, however what is not disputed is that this legislation will result in a massive growth in federal spending which will substantially increase the national debt, as well as the fact that the cost of the legislation will require tax increases which will further burden the economy. We all know that there is no free lunch. No one believes that the federal government can provide anything more efficiently than the free market. It never has and it never will. The mistake of Obamacare was that instead of trying to create a "safety-net" plan for the minority of our citizens who are uninsured, this plan federalizes the entire healthcare industry. If you have any common sense, you know that will be more costly, less efficient and agonizingly bureaucratic.

President Obama is a liberal, big government solutions oriented politician with a strong resemblance to a socialist. President Obama believes that the best way to solve problems in our country is to give complete control over the problems to the federal government, and to empower the government to manage more and more of our daily lives. His way of doing things does not work and it will ultimately destroy our economy and diminish the living standards of all Americans.

Oh, and one more thing. Is anything ever his own fault, or responsibility? George W. Bush hasn't been the President for three years! Obama blames everything that is not going well on George W. Bush. Really Mr. Obama? After three years in office, it is time that you started taking responsibility for your actions and for your failed and failing programs and policies. George W. Bush did not give us the $825 billion Stimulus program that did not work. George W. Bush did not give us Obamacare, which will run up the national debt and will lower the quality of healthcare received by our senior citizens. George W. Bush did not start a regulatory assault on the energy industry that has nearly doubled gasoline prices, killed thousands of jobs in the domestic petroleum industry, and is threatening to substantially diminish the coal industry in this nation.

So here and now I will say it: FIRE OBAMA!! Barack Obama MUST NOT BE RE-ELECTED! You must not vote for this man in November 2012. This man is not ignorant or misguided. He is fully aware of what he is doing. He is fully understanding that his policies are not improving the economy and that ultimately his policies will continue to do harm to the economy. He is an ideologue. He has to deceive you about his intentions in order to gain your vote.   I am going to give you five specific reasons why re-electing Barack Obama will greatly harm our country, and reduce the standard of living of most American citizens. Please read on.

Chapter Two

The debt bomb

The United States Government is in a financial crisis. This crisis is in the early stages and can still be corrected if proper actions are taken. The proper actions, in summary would include some real spending cuts and some revenue growth. The spending cuts can be accomplished through some disciplined planning, however will also require the overhaul of some very high profile programs. To make big progress on what is a very big problem, will require the willingness to change the biggest spending programs. President Obama has no intention of addressing these programs, or fixing this growing debt problem. If he did, he would be talking about these solutions. He is not. And he will not. The needed revenue increases must be accomplished via growth of the economy which will generate incrementally more tax revenue, which can be incentivized through business friendly and pro-growth tax policy and a less heavy handed regulatory environment. Tax revenue will not grow and remain sustainable through marginal tax rate increases.

Our government has a total debt of $15.7 trillion dollars, and growing. As a number 15.7 trillion looks like 15,700,000,000,000. That is a number that is so big it is hard for the average person to have perspective. Well, let me give you some perspective. This is the most debt that the nation has ever had, not only as a real number, but also in relation to the size of the economy. That is the part that should scare you. The debt in relation to the size of our economy helps you understand whether we can afford to repay the debt or not. In our history, the national debt was a small percentage of the GDP (less than 50%) from 1900 to 1940. In the first half of the 1940s, when we were fighting World War II, federal spending exploded and as a result so did the national debt. The national debt actually exceeded 100% of the nation's GDP in 1945. However after the war ended, federal spending decreased because we didn't have to produce so much military hardware. Thus after the war, total federal spending actually decreased. Also there was great economic expansion in the late

40's and in the 50's so the national debt as a percentage of the GDP steadily declined to below 50%by 1965. The debt remained under 50% until the late 1980's. Then the debt began to grow because of federal budget deficits (we spent more money than we raised in tax revenue).

In 2000 the U.S. federal debt totaled approximately 70%of the annual GDP. From that point forward federal spending began a dramatic increase that pushed the total debt to a higher percentage compared to GDP every year, until at the end of 2008, the national debt topped 100% of the annual GDP, for the first time since the end of World War II in 1945! In 2011, our federal government raised $2.5 trillion in tax revenue. And in 2011 our federal government spent $3.8 trillion. So in 2011 alone, the federal government added $1.3 trillion to the national debt. That is 8.6% of our total national debt added in just one year! Stop and think about that for a moment. It is significant, and really it is scary. Considering that our nation is 236 years old, that is a huge prorata of new debt in just one fiscal year. It is in fact, shocking. Again, these numbers are so large that it is difficult to comprehend. So let's put it in the perspective of an average American family.

The median annual family income in the U.S. at the end of 2011 was $51,400. If this "median" American family lived a life style fueled by deficit spending at the same rate as the U.S. government has recently, it would mean that in 2012 when they earned $51,400, they would have spent $77,520. If the family is spending more than they make, then they have to pay the deficit portion of the bills by using a credit card. So after one year the family has a credit card bill with a balance of $26,520. That is a lot of credit card debt for a family to carry (not pay off), but they are not finished. If the credit card still has an unused credit limit, and the family spends $1.50 for every $1.00 that they earn for a second year, then the credit card bill increases to $53,040. Actually the balance will be even higher because in the second year the family has to make payments on the credit card, and since they are spending more than they make, then they are effectively borrowing their credit card payments from the credit card.

Now every year that the family continues this behavior, and that they don't bring their spending down to the level of their income, the credit card debt balance goes higher and higher. This means that the amount of the debt payment gets higher, so as the debt service payments increase the family has less money to spend on the mortgage, car payments, groceries and discretionary spending. So the critical question for the family is, how high is the borrowing limit on the credit card? Unless the family cuts spending, or dramatically increases their income, there will come a limit to their borrowing. The question is how long does this "party" last? And what happens when they reach that limit? When they reach the borrowing limit and there is no more deficit spending, then the family has to take drastic steps to cut the total annual spending to be at or lower than their level of income. So they will have to cut their standard of living because they have lived beyond their means for so long. They will have to move to a smaller home, and/or go from two cars down to one car. Maybe they can't afford any vacations. The bottom line is, because the family was irresponsible with their spending and lived beyond their means they will have to bear some uncomfortable budget cutting, or else there will be some very bad financial consequences (i.e. foreclosure, repossession, etc.).

The United States government does not have unlimited borrowing ability. Our ability to borrow is related directly to our ability to repay our debt. As the debt becomes higher relative to the government's annual tax revenue, then the theoretical "credit limit" starts to become an issue. The U.S. government has a credit rating, similar to you personally, and to American businesses. When your credit rating is good, everyone wants to lend to you. But as your credit rating declines due to high debt levels, you may find lenders less willing to lend more money to you. Or they may require a higher interest rate. Our government faces this same situation.

In August of 2011 Standard & Poor's downgraded the credit rating of the U.S. Federal Government for the first time ever. Repeat: the credit rating of the U.S. Federal Government has been downgraded for the first time, ever!! In chapter one we talked about the corporate CEO whose results were so bad that he got fired. Remember? Well, our CEO, the President has just presided over the first downgrading of the nation's credit rating ever. So I ask, what is President Obama doing about the first credit downgrade ever? Is he proposing spending cuts, program reductions and prioritization. No! He is not doing any of these things. In fact, he is moving forward with his entire deficit spending agenda. He has no regard for the problem and its obvious consequences. I'll say it again, just like our wayward corporate CEO of the first chapter, OBAMA MUST BE FIRED (in November via the election).

Here is another little tidbit of information that you need to be aware of. The amount of money that the federal government has to pay on the debt is dependent upon the interest rates. Right now interest rates are at an all-time low. Even with interest rates at all-time lows, the interest expense on the U.S. debt in fiscal year 2011 was $454 billion, the highest in U.S. history. That is nearly 25% of the tax revenue generated in 2011. And that is just interest. No principal repayment included. If interest rates increase then the interest expense will increase also. This is what I meant by the title "the debt bomb". The debt is a bomb that can blow up in our face and cripple the nation economically. More than half of the U.S. debt has a maturity date of less than one year. The total debt has an average maturity of three years. So if interest rates begin to rise, the impact will be felt on the federal budget nearly immediately. With the banking and governmental crisis that is currently unfolding in western Europe, it is just a matter of time before interest rates will rise. Greater risk always drives up interest rates. The rates can be kept low by government economic policy manipulation for only so long. If the interest expense increases substantially, and it will if rates rise, then the nation will have less money available to pay for necessary programs such as Medicare, Medicaid, Social Security, the national defense and other basic services provided by the federal government. The debt bomb is probably the most important issue in this election. This has the potential to cripple this nation. Obama has no plan to deal with the debt. Obama has no intention to make a plan to deal with the debt. This makes him a very bad President, unworthy of the office that he seeks to re-occupy. If you are a responsible citizen, you love your country, and you want the future generations of Americans to live a good life with free market opportunity like you have, then you must do the right thing in November and FIRE OBAMA.

In this chapter two "The debt bomb" I have talked about the size of the debt, how fast it is growing, and the cost of the debt. I have warned that there are devastating consequences for the nation's economy, which of course means you the American citizen, if we don't do something to stop the rapid growth of the debt. So now I want to show you what will happen to us if we don't fix this problem, for which step one is to FIRE OBAMA.

There are some current day examples of country's that have lived beyond their means, and have run up so much debt that now their economies are crippled by the debt load. Terrible things are happening to their citizens as a result. So let's review a current day example of what can happen to the U.S. unless we fix our debt problem.

We will look at Greece. The Greek government spent beyond its means for years, just as the U.S. has been doing since 2000. The deficit spending caused Greece to borrow more money than it collected in tax revenue.

Their debt is well over 100% of the country's GDP (as is the U.S.), and now

(since 2011) Greece would have literally defaulted on its debt, if not for

some short term "bail outs" provided by some bailout creditors. The Greek

government is now living day-to-day on the tax revenues that it collects,

because they cannot borrow any more money. There is no one willing to

lend further to Greece because they cannot repay the debt that they

already have. As a result life for the average Greek citizen has become

very difficult. Nearly 20% of the Greek economy is based on government

funding, for public employees, administration, defense, education, health

services, social security and public pensions. For years public employees

have been promised generous pensions upon retirement. The government

has historically been bloated and inefficient (does that sound familiar

America?). When the western European economy entered a recession in

2008, the Greek economy did as well and has been in recession since (for

5 years). With their heavy debt load, the Greek government had no chance

of repaying their debt as it came due. The Greek government has had to

institute austerity measures because of their liquidity crisis (no money).

These measures include: cuts in healthcare spending and pharmaceutical benefits (Greece has socialized healthcare – aka "Obamacare" – hello, America); cuts in public investment (roads and other infrastructure); cuts in defense; cuts in public retiree pension benefits, both existing and future; and reductions in central government employees. All of these reductions are absolutely necessary, but they also translate to hardship for many Greek citizens. The unemployment rate in Greece is over 20%, and for those age 25 and below, unemployment is over 30%. This devastating economic crisis has caused major social upheaval on the streets of Greek cities, as there has been rioting and looting in protest of the government austerity moves. This could have been avoided if the government had managed its affairs responsibly. Because they didn't, it will take years, if not decades to recover from the hole that Greece has dug for itself.

"Those who do not know history are destined to repeat it" (Edmund Burke). The U.S. has examples of social welfare based governments, and the economic consequences that ultimately ensue. Greece is one. And there are others. If you do not want to see the U.S. go the way of Greece, then use your common sense and FIRE OBAMA in November.

Greece is a horror story. It is a worst case scenario. However, it is a real world example of what can happen to the U.S. unless we take action to stop the rapid and massive accumulation of debt. To emphasize the recent acceleration of the debt, here is a helpful eye chart:

United States Federal Government
(millions of dollars)

Year	Federal Revenue	% change	Federal Spending	% change	Federal DEBT	% change
2000	2,025,198		1,788,950		5,625,700	
2001	1,991,142	-1.7%	1,862,846	4.1%	5,769,881	2.6%
2002	1,853,149	-6.9%	2,010,894	7.9%	6,198,401	7.4%
2003	1,782,321	-3.8%	2,159,899	7.4%	6,760,014	9.1%
2004	1,880,126	5.5%	2,292,841	6.2%	7,354,657	8.8%
2005	2,153,625	14.5%	2,471,957	7.8%	7,905,300	7.5%
2006	2,406,876	11.8%	2,655,050	7.4%	8,451,350	6.9%
2007	2,568,001	6.7%	2,728,686	2.8%	8,950,744	5.9%
2008	2,523,991	-1.7%	2,982,544	9.3%	9,986,082	11.6%
2009	2,104,989	-16.6%	3,517,677	17.9%	11,875,851	18.9%
2010	2,162,724	2.7%	3,456,213	-1.7%	13,528,807	13.9%
2011	2,303,466	6.5%	3,603,061	4.2%	15,125,899	11.8%

Source: Office of Management and Budget

The numbers in the chart do not lie. So, in the first 224 years of the nation's history we accumulated $5.6 billion in national debt. Then, in the 10 years from 2001 through 2011 the government ran up $9.5 billion in additional debt. We tripled our debt in 10 years!! The national debt has grown more in Obama's three years than in all eight years of President Bush. Yet Obama has no plan to deal with the problem. Even though the exploding debt is the largest problem facing the American economy, Obama has not made reducing the annual budget deficit, and controlling the growth of the national debt a priority. *That is outrageous! Do I have your attention yet?* This is a national crisis, and the President who wants you to re-elect him is not dealing with it at all. In fact, if he is re-elected his policies will make the problem worse!!

Here is a common sense budget question for you to think about. Look back on the prior page at the eye chart. Notice the large increase in spending going from 2008 to 2009. This was caused by the 2009 $800 billion stimulus package. If the stimulus bill was only approved for 2009, then why did the government spending not go back down in 2010? The answer is, your government basically lies to you about the budget and in particular about the spending. The way that they do it and get away with it is by using a trick called "base line budgeting". This started with the Congressional Budget Act of 1974. It ensures that unless there is a specific and intentional budget cut passed by law, that every line item in the budget each year will start at the prior year's amount, and then increase for inflation. So even if Congress does nothing (does not approve a new budget for the new year), there will be the prior year's budget amount plus an inflation increase in all budget line items. This is how government spending gets out of control. Some line items in the budget may be for programs that are for one year. Or the line item may be a bigger priority in one year than another. However, with base line budgeting once funds are in the budget, they don't decrease. In fact they increase every year by inflation. *INSANE!!*

The way that your government officials essentially lie to you about "budget cuts" is to use the trick of base line budgeting: if a particular budget item is increased from $100 to $200 in a given year, but in that year they only spend $150, then they will claim to have cut spending by $50 (because they didn't spend the entire budget amount). Spending wasn't cut by $50, it was raised by $50 (prior year you spent $100; this year you spent $150). The only way to fix this is to make the government live on zero based budgeting. This is how you and I live our everyday lives. You budget based on the amount of money that you have available to spend, not based on a projection (wish list) that has no relation to available resources (tax revenue).

I believe that most Americans who read this debt information will be shocked at how quickly our situation has gotten out of hand, and just how bad it is. My hope is that the Americans who read this and give it some thought, will understand that it is their future that is at stake. It is their responsibility to do something to cause this situation to be changed. The man that we (America) elected to lead our country is not leading our country on a path of prosperity. He is leading the country down a path of false messages about social welfare and "social justice". I have demonstrated to you in this chapter with the facts, what the results will be if we continue down this President's path. It leads to financial ruin and desperation for many of our citizens. We have to stop it. The first step is to remove Obama from office in November. So be sure that you are registered to vote, and go to your polling place on Tuesday November 6 and vote Obama out of office. Not convinced yet? Well then, I will give you more reasons why Barack Obama should not be our President for four more years.

Chapter Three

Energy: America needs it – Obama is abusing it

If you live in the following states, and you vote for Obama in November, you are literally voting against job creation, and for the destruction of the energy industry (and jobs) in your state: Texas, Alaska, California, North Dakota, Wyoming, Oklahoma, Louisiana, New Mexico, Montana, Pennsylvania, West Virginia, Utah, Ohio, Kentucky, Washington, New Jersey, Michigan, Tennessee, Mississippi, Colorado, Arkansas, Alabama, Illinois, Minnesota, Kansas, Arizona. These 26 states are either prominent in, or important to the production and/or refining of oil, coal or natural gas for the domestic energy industry. Note to Obama and the environmentalists: If you think that there is sufficient supply or technology of any alternative source of energy at an affordable cost, then you have no grasp on the reality of the real world that the rest of the tax payers are living in. And the results of the "Green Energy" federal spending in the last three years is the evidence of this fact.

Aside from the debt bomb, the availability of abundant and affordable energy resources is the most critical issue for the well-being of the American economy. Most U.S. citizens would agree with that statement. It is just common sense. However, if you look at how Obama has made decisions as President with regard to energy policy, and how his administration is using the Environmental Protection Agency (EPA) to its political ideology ends, then you will have to conclude that Obama is not in favor of a healthy domestic energy industry. No kidding. This is another example of how this man is failing, and how he plans to fail even more. And I will just say it again... Energy policy is another reason why we must FIRE OBAMA IN NOVEMBER!! Let me say this, I believe that Jimmy Carter is the worst President that the U.S. has ever had, although Obama is a close second. But Obama is the most energy industry unfriendly President that we have had since Jimmy Carter. Does Jimmy Carter ever have anything good to say about the United States? OK, I am sorry, I digress.

The reason for my reference to Jimmy Carter, is that Obama is making the same mistake that the peanut farmer from Georgia made. Carter formed his energy policy on the assumption that hydrocarbon energy resources were literally becoming extinct. The only hydrocarbon resources that were actually depleting were the "low hanging fruit" that had been the "early finds". Carter did not allow for the possibility of new and developing technology which would lead to the development of new and undiscovered energy sources. Rather than formulate policies that would incentivize the energy industry experts to explore for and develop new energy resources, Carter reacted like a typical liberal, and legislated the energy issue as if the federal government had the only answers. It had disastrous results for the American economy. Ultimately Carter and his administration were proved wrong and the U.S. energy industry has developed significant new resources. Now Obama is making the same mistake as Carter, but for completely different reasons. Carter was about fear and conservation. Obama is all about environmental ideology.

I think that Carter actually meant well, but he had no faith in American free market dynamics. He thought like a big government liberal. He acted like a protectionist, rather than an entrepreneur. Now, Obama is a different story. He is literally intentionally trying to harm the American energy industry, in the sense that he wants prices for fossil fuels to rise precipitously. For him this is an issue that is a key part of his ideology. I said earlier at the end of chapter one that Obama is a big government liberal with a strong resemblance to a socialist. To make matters worse for our country, he is also a dedicated extreme environmentalist. He is so dedicated to his extreme left wing liberal beliefs, that he has and will continue to, legislate in ways that are clearly harmful to the economic well-being of the U.S. economy and our fellow citizens. If this does not make you angry. then you are just not paying attention! I am going to spend this chapter discussing how Obama is harming the industries that provide coal, oil, natural gas and electricity to American industries and for our citizens. This issue alone should make the election in November a landslide (against Obama of course!).

Let's first discuss "big oil". Big oil is a term that is meant to cast the oil industry in a negative light. The reality is that oil is the primary energy source that fuels the engine of commerce in our country and for the entire world's economy. Our economy cannot function without it. And despite what you may hear from the leftist environmentalists, there is a relatively plentiful supply of oil. Our government has the ability to irrationally affect the price that you pay for energy, and even has the ability to completely cripple the industry.

In April 2012 a video was discovered of an EPA official who was making some remarks that indicated just how much Obama's EPA intends to do harm to the American energy industry. The video shows EPA Region IV Administrator Al Armendariz describe his agency's "philosophy of enforcement" with respect to the regulation of oil and gas companies, comparing it to brutal tactics that were employed by the ancient Roman army to intimidate its foes into submission. With a sarcastic tone and expression, Armendariz detailed the joy with which the EPA inflicts punishment on the oil industry: "It was kind of like how the Romans used to, you know, conquer the villages in the Mediterranean. They would go into a little Turkish town somewhere and they would find the first five guys they saw and they would crucify them. And then, you know, that town was really easy to manage for the next few years". This sarcastic statement reveals just how the extremist environmental officials in the Obama administration and in the EPA view their ability to influence operations of the oil industry. According to Armendariz, the EPA views its enforcement efforts as a violent crucifixion intended to intimidate and influence companies into submission. This does not surprise me, though I am sure that this EPA official regrets that his statement made it in to the public's awareness. As I said earlier, the Obama administration is the most anti-energy administration in history. For President Obama and his team of bureaucrats, "Big Oil" is the enemy that deserves to be beaten into submission. Of course, you are never going to hear Obama talk this way publicly. He cannot reveal to you the voter just what his true intentions are. If he did he wouldn't have any chance in the general election. But if you just look at his record since he has been in office, it is easy to tell what his policy intentions really are. Oh, by the way Al Armendariz resigned his position with the EPA, and shortly thereafter joined the Sierra Club, an environmental activist group. It is not surprising to see a big government environmental activist go to the home of environmental activism. And if there was one confirmed liberally biased administrator in the EPA, you can be sure that there are a lot of them still there, doing Obama's bidding.

The reality is that the key to an abundance of affordable energy resources is maximum exploration. There is a clear and understandable illustration of this. The U.S. has approximately 2.5% of the world's provable oil reserves. However the U.S. produces approximately 9% of the world's oil. This makes the U.S. the world's third largest oil producer behind Russia and Saudi Arabia. If the U.S. has only 2.5% of provable reserves how does the U.S. produce so much oil? The answer is that the U.S. has the most efficient, effective and creative domestic oil industry in the world. The U.S. oil industry produces what it finds and it explores and finds even more.

Here is further illustration of the success of American oil exploration. In 1990 U.S. provable oil reserves totaled approximately 34 billion barrels. In 2010 U.S. provable oil reserves totaled approximately 31 billion barrels. In the 20 years in between the U.S. domestic oil industry produced 52 billion barrels of oil. So the industry produced nearly twice as much as the previously provable reserves, yet the provable reserves only declined by 3 billion barrels (10%) in 20 years. How is this possible? Innovation and technology development. The free market at work. The U.S. oil industry is the most innovative domestic industry in the world.

The U.S. oil and gas industry has been amazingly productive in finding, producing and refining this country's mineral assets. The U.S. free market and ingenuity has shown that it is not the size of the reserve that matters, but it is what you can do with it. In the past century the oil and gas production industry has gone from primarily wildcatters operating basically on "a hunch", to an industry where the most modern seismic and geosteering technologies allow drillers to steer their drill bits so accurately that they can literally hit within inches of the target that is two miles, or more beneath the surface of the earth. Remarkable! This is the kind of technological development that Jimmy Carter just could not foresee, or trust the free market to develop.

The real problem with Obama's approach to energy policy is his underlying ideology. President Obama is a true believer in such liberal environmental issues as man-made global warming, cap and trade and the "carbon footprint". President Obama wants to force American consumers to use less energy at any cost, because he believes that it is wrong for America to consume fossil fuels. His choice for Secretary of Energy, Steven Chu, said in a 2008 interview "we have to figure out how to boost the price of gasoline to the levels in Europe". For those of you who do not know, that is approximately $10/gallon. Can you imagine what that would do to the American economy? Steven Chu was the President's choice for Energy Secretary, so you can trust that Obama agrees with his opinion. Chu is after all, still the Energy secretary three years after that statement. These people are environmentalists. Obama is not going to come out and campaign this way. If he did you would not vote for him. But just look at his policies, and how abrogatingly the EPA regulates the energy industry. Obama had all new drilling shut down in the gulf of Mexico after the BP incident for one full year. Some period of delay of new well drilling was probably warranted to ensure prevention of another accident similar to the "BP Deepwater Horizon" incident. However, a full year of closure to new drilling was an opportunistic policy by the anti-energy industry Obama administration. Furthermore, after the delay was lifted, permitting is extremely slow. So slow that a spokesman for the American Petroleum Institute stated "we look forward to the day when a single permit on plan does not merit a press conference by the Secretary of the Interior".

The Obama administration is doing everything in its power to terminate, curtail or prevent drilling for oil anywhere in or near the United States, including Alaska and the Gulf of Mexico. The Interior Secretary is blocking new permits, and finding ways to prevent the approval process to move forward. This is because the virulently environmentalist Obama administration does not believe in oil drilling, especially anywhere near the United States. Environmentalists don't want oil drilling and they don't care that this reduces supply and raises prices. In fact, as we know (i.e. Secretary Chu's statement) they want prices to rise. Rising prices mean people in general will buy less gas. People buying less gas means less energy is consumed, and the earth is closer to its pristine and also barbaric state that environmentalists irrationally desire.

If you need further evidence of Obama's anti-energy industry, and pro radical environmentalist policy leanings, then just look at his decision regarding the proposed Keystone XL oil pipeline from Canada to the United States. This proposed pipeline would provide approximately 20,000 construction jobs in the United States to build the pipeline. There would also be permanent jobs to maintain and operate the pipeline, as well as residual jobs along the pipeline route in the communities that support these proposed workers. And then of course there is the fact that the pipeline would permanently increase the supply of oil from our friendly neighbor Canada, and offer an alternative to the middle east oil that is always at risk from the radical Islamic threat. This pipeline would provide jobs in a high unemployment environment, and would increase domestic oil supply at a time of critical energy supply and price issues. And Obama rejected it. Why? Come on people, if this isn't obvious to you then you are drinking, or smoking something. This is a play by Obama to appease the environmental policies he desires, and of course the environmentalist lobby that supports him. If your priority is to increase the supply of affordable energy to the U.S. economy, and to provide good paying jobs to available skilled American workers, then this pipeline is a no brainer! You support it. Well America, your President, Barack Obama does not support it and he killed it for now (until 2013, after the election). And if he is re-elected, he will kill it for as long as he is in power to do so. That is just economically insane, and further evidence that we must FIRE OBAMA in November!

Here is some further evidence of Obama's legislative and regulatory war on the domestic oil industry. Obama has targeted "big oil", one of the strongest job-creating sectors of the U.S. economy, in his proposed 2013 fiscal year budget with multiple new or increased taxes. (Economics 101 will show that increasing taxes is a job growth killer) For the fourth consecutive year Obama is proposing to repeal Section 199 of the

"American Jobs Creation Act". If repealed, it will increase taxes on oil and natural gas companies by an estimated $12 billion over the next decade. It could possibly jeopardize some of the millions of American jobs supported by natural gas producers and discourage new job growth in the industry due to reduced working capital. The Section 199 tax deduction is currently available to all U.S. manufacturing firms on their "qualifying income" from domestic production, at a rate of 9 percent. The oil and gas industry is already only allowed to deduct 6 percent, due to previous legislation.

The Obama budget additionally targets oil and natural gas companies for higher taxes by proposing to repeal: (1) expensing intangible drilling costs; (2) "last in-first out" (LIFO) accounting in favor of the higher taxed "first in-first out" accounting methodology; (3) the deduction for tertiary injectants (fluids, gases and chemicals) that are used in unconventional drilling, and (4) the percentage depletion allowance to recover for capital investments. Additional tax increases on the oil and natural gas industry will come from proposed modifications of the dual capacity rule (a U.S. tax policy that prevents the double taxation of foreign earnings), which increases the amortization period for exploration costs, and finally by reinstating Superfund taxes. All combined, it is projected by the American Petroleum Institute that all eight targeted proposals of the Obama fiscal year 2013 budget would hit the oil and gas industry with almost $86 billion in higher taxes over the next ten years. Energy companies have been aggressively expandng operations in domestic oil and natural gas fields in North Dakota, and from Texas to Pennsylvania, and they may be incentivized to shift their operations to foreign exploration if U.S. tax policies make it less profitable to operate in domestic oil and natural gas exploration and drilling. These companies are in business to make a profit for their owners and investors, and will do so by making prudent business decisions based on economic challenges, opportunities and incentives.

Now let's shift gears to another energy source that Obama is attacking. This one hits really close to home for all of us, literally. If you pay an electric bill you better pay close attention to this. The issue is coal. Somewhere near one-half of the electric power plants in America are coal fired. That is a good thing, because America is the "Saudi Arabia" of coal.

We have a lot of it. The supply is projected at approximately 200 years-worth. And coal is relatively inexpensive. Advances have been made in the technology of burning the coal to supply energy, to make it much less impactful on the environment. Emissions have been reduced to the point that coal powered plants are capturing over 99 percent of particulate emissions released during the combustion process. However, Obama and his "green" buddies don't see it that way, and he has radical plans for coal powered electric plants. He intends to eliminate them. And soon. This will have drastic consequences for the economy and the U.S. power grid.

Let me be clear. Obama intends to greatly limit and minimize the coal industry in America. Obama made a comment in 2008 with regard to his plans for coal fueled power plants: "if somebody wants to build a coal fueled power plant they can; it's just that it will bankrupt them, because they are going to be charged a huge tax for the greenhouse gas they produce". The greenhouse gas is CO2, carbon dioxide. You and every creature on earth emits this gas when you breathe. There is no hard scientific proof that human activity is causing "global warming". The earth's climate has varied up and down throughout time, even before man inhabited the earth. Man-made global warming is a theory supported by environmentalists, and they try to bend science to support their point of view. Obama buys this point of view fully. So he plans to cripple an industry with no regard to the impact on the American economy and American jobs. His first strategy for accomplishing this was through legislation. The "cap and trade" bill was passed by the House of Representatives, however it was not passed by the Senate. But that did not deter Obama. What he cannot accomplish through legislation, he will just accomplish through regulation. And damn the opinion of the American public. He is not a President. He is a King! And he must go, so FIRE HIM IN NOVEMBER.

About 40 percent of the U.S. electric grid supply is generated by coal powered plants. The EPA has instituted environmental standards called the Utility MACT (Maximum Achievable Control Technology) targeted to regulate electric power plants. These new standards take effect in 2015, and will result in the closing of many coal powered plants that generate approximately 40 percent of the current available capacity in the U.S.

power grid. The industry is very concerned about the ability to retrofit environmental controls or to build replacement capacity in the three years to comply with the Utility MACT rules. These rules have been characterized as a regulatory "train wreck" that will impose excessive costs and lead to plant retirements that will threaten the adequacy of electric grid capacity (reliability of supply) across the country. Furthermore, the average American electric bill will increase 10 to 20 percent, depending on what segment of the country that you live in, and the relative dependence on coal power versus newer technologies. An increase of 10 to 20 percent may not sound like much, but if you are living on a fixed income, as many seniors and low income earners do, then any increase is substantial. And this increase is avoidable!

The reliability of the nation's electric generating system is at risk because of the number of new rules and regulations applicable to power plants. The stringency of these regulations, the lack of flexibility within these regulations, and the severe compliance schedules that are required put power grid reliability at risk. Accelerated plant retirements and shutdowns that will be triggered by the Utility MACT rule will cause reserve capacity to decline, increasing the likelihood, severity and longevity of electric service interruptions (brown-outs and black-outs).

Because of the unrealistic compliance timelines in the new EPA rules utility operators will have to prematurely shut down as much as 25 percent of the current coal-fueled generating capacity, which will cause the elimination of thousands of good power plant jobs. The primary impacts of many of the rules will largely be on coal fired plants more than 40 years old that have not installed state of the art pollution controls. Many of these plants are inefficient and will eventually be replaced by more efficient and environmentally friendly coal or natural gas plants, a development most likely to be encouraged if the price of the primary competing fuel, natural gas, continues to be low. The point is that in due time the market factors would have replaced the oldest and least clean burning coal plants due to their age and the improvement of the new technology. This could have been achieved without the trauma and the risk to the sufficiency of the nation's power grid. However, the radical extreme environmental lobby that is supported by Obama demanded this heavy-handed and immediate action, which Obama provided with regulation through the EPA, after being denied by legislative actions. So the well-being of the American economy is being ignored. Why should that surprise us after our discussion of the "debt bomb". This President is an ideologue and is focused solely on his agenda with no regard for the American people. It is why we must FIRE OBAMA in November! If you cannot see this, you are either not listening or you are just not reachable.

Now let's talk about the area of energy policy where Barack Obama really defines himself as a liberal environmentalist, and where he is most like Jimmy Carter in that he does not trust the market place to define the products and services of the day. He is trying to force his ideological solutions via big government policy. "Green energy".

In the fall of 2008 Obama said "We'll invest $150 billion over the next decade and harness private efforts to build a clean-energy economy". That is an average of $15 billion per year of tax payer money. And he said that this would create 5 million new jobs that pay well, and that can never be outsourced. (uh…yeah, right) The "green jobs" predictions are turning out to be a pipe dream. The President's stimulus bill included tens of millions of dollars in new government subsidies for politically favored renewable-energy interests; $6 billion in loan guarantees for renewable energy companies; $17 billion for the Department of Energy's energy efficiency and renewable energy programs; $2 billion for energy-efficient battery manufacturing; and billions more on other "clean energy" programs, for a total of $30 billion. $80,000,000,000!

The federal government's job is to make and enforce the rules of the road, so that markets are fair, transparent and competitive; to foster an environment that is conducive to private-sector job creation. Obama's approach has been characterized by punitive regulations on commercially competitive sources of energy, combined with reckless spending on uncompetitive and partially unviable alternatives. Instead of promoting the innovative and entrepreneurial genius of the American free market, the

President's agenda has placed decision making in Washington through a "toxic mix" of higher spending and more crippling regulations.

We have seen this before. In the late 1970's, in response to oil embargos, the Carter Administration championed the development of synthetic fuels and ethanol. One memorable failure pushed by the Carter White House was the Synthetic Fuels Corporation, intended to finance the development of commercial synthetic fuel plants through massive government subsidies. After subjecting the taxpayers to more than $400 billion in subsidies, this government created corporation closed its doors in 1986.

Since its introduction in the 2009 stimulus bill, the Department of Energy has issued $40 billion in new loan guarantees for private sector loans for renewable energy projects that may not have otherwise been market viable. Already several of these multi-million dollar projects initially labeled as successes, have failed. The most notorious was a solar start-up company, Solyndra, which received a $535 million loan guarantee in the fall of 2009, after repeated warnings from federal financial analysts about the company's risk of failure. Within two years of the loan guarantee and funding, Solyndra filed bankruptcy and laid off 1,100 employees only 15 months after Obama's now infamous photo-op at the company's factory. Even in the midst of this and other failures the Department of Energy has continued to advertise additional loan guarantee recipients, announcing a $1.2 billion loan guarantee to another solar company just one day after the FBI raided Solyndra's offices!

Advocates of green energy have long argued that it is not enough for the government to subsidize alternative energy sources; it also needs to promote policies that make commercially competitive sources of energy more expensive. We know that Obama buys in to that thought process! This is the idea behind the controversial "cap and trade" bill that President Obama tried to pass through Congress in 2009. It was defeated, and instead of accepting the verdict on his ideological policy, the administration decided to use the Environmental Protection Agency (EPA) to carry out a unilateral plan to impose emissions restrictions on American businesses.

Here's the deal, I am not against the idea of green energy. I would absolutely love to think that one day we can have an unlimited supply of affordable electricity generated from the sun, or the wind, and with no pollution by-product. That would be awesome and we all want that. But how realistic is it? With existing technology, it is not realistic. Not right now. The way to get to that energy dream land is not by government funded shots in the dark. The government can play a productive role in the development of new energy sources, but it will be through incentivizing the free market with tax and investment credits. The creativeness in the entrepreneurs of the free market, combined with the risk takers in the capital markets, will make innovation happen. Just look at the inventive history of this great country and economy since the beginning of the 20th century. It was not driven by intervention of the federal government! It was driven by entrepreneurial spirit and the free market resources of the United States economy. Mr. Obama should learn from studying history. It repeats. For better or for worse.

Finally, I want to issue a challenge to 10 states, that are prominent domestic energy producing states, and that went for Obama in 2008. The future of your job market in the energy industry is at stake in this election. Literally. If you go for Obama you are insuring the further loss of energy segment jobs in your state! These 10 states are:

New Mexico;   Pennsylvania;   Ohio;   Michigan;   New Jersey; Washington;   Minnesota;   Illinois;   Colorado;   and last but not least California!   That's right I said it;   California!!!   This is a critical election. The future of our country and of the job market in your states, is at risk. You must review these critical, factual issues and do the right thing. FIRE OBAMA IN NOVEMBER.   Your future and the future of your children depends upon it.

Chapter Four

Healthcare – Socialism

I told you at the end of chapter one that President Obama is a liberal, big government solutions oriented politician with a strong resemblance to a socialist. In this chapter we will discuss an issue that is socialism, and it is Obama's signature legislation. It will be his legacy. Government mandated healthcare. This is socialism. It is a slippery slope for our government and for our society. The idea of dependence on the government for your well-being. The federal government will now, by law, mandate that everyone purchase health insurance. What is next, mandate that homeless people buy a house? I mean really, if the government can mandate and tax everything, then there is no limit to their whims in a "social view".

This is a very controversial subject. The idea of every citizen in the country having health insurance is as utopian as the idea of turning solar energy in to usable and affordable electric power with no pollution. It is a wonderful concept and a noble goal. But to say that you can do it without a substantial cost is just naïve, and quite frankly dishonest. This program (Obamacare) is the biggest government power grab in the history of the country. It represents the largest tax increase in the history of the world! It is a tax increase, and was defined as such by the Supreme Court in their ruling to uphold the Obamacare legislation.

I have mentioned to you previously that if Obama was fully honest with the public about what his real intentions are, he would never get elected. He has to deceive the voters and convince them that he is doing something other than what will be the real results of his policies. From the beginning Obama has been less than honest about what the real outcome of Obamacare would be. Let's go back and look at what his campaign promises for Obamacare were. There were a lot of promises, so this may seem like rambling, but stay with me.

These are some of the statements and descriptions of the proposed government healthcare plan from the Obama campaign: Quality, affordable and portable coverage for all; new health initiatives, including for autism and aids; lower costs for the U.S. health care system, including lower drug costs.   Obama will make available a new national health plan to all Americans, including the self-employed and small businesses, to buy affordable health coverage that is similar to the plan available to members of Congress. ** {editorial comment by the author: The average citizen will never get anything that members of Congress get.}   No pre-existing conditions. Comprehensive benefits: the benefit package will include all essential medical services, including preventive, maternity and mental health care. Affordable premiums, co-pays and deductibles. Under "the plan", if you like your current health insurance, nothing changes, except that your costs will go down by as much as $2,500 per year.   No family making less than $250,000 a year will see any form of tax increase.

OK, enough already. Those of you out there who have some common sense and are willing to use it know that when someone promises you something for nothing, you had better hold on to your pocket book. We who live in the real world know that there is no "free lunch". And the reality of "Obamacare" is that this program is not really about health insurance for people who don't have it. Obama is using healthcare as a vehicle to allow the federal government to control the lives of the American people. It is the utopia of liberalism; socialism.

A majority of Americans are opposed to Obamacare as it has been legislated. The polling ranges from 50 to 60 percent against Obamacare, depending on how the questions are asked. The polling also indicates that real support for Obamacare is only 25 to 35 percent. These are people who really think that they are getting something for nothing. They believe that "government healthcare" is being paid for by someone else. But they are so wrong about that. The majority of the cost of Obamacare is to be paid for by middle class and low income people. That is the whole point of the individual mandate. Everyone is required to "buy" health insurance.

Obamacare is the nickname assigned to legislation passed by the Congress and signed by President Obama in March 2010, entitled "The patient Protection and Affordable Care Act". This is without question the most over-reaching legislation enacted in to law in U.S. history. This singular legislation will transform the United States to a socialist society. It will do great harm to the economy, because the worst thing that you can do during a recession or stagnant growth economy is to increase taxation. Since Obamacare has been upheld by the Supreme Court, the only answer is to FIRE OBAMA in November, and to repeal the Obamacare legislation through Congressional action.

The title "Patient Protection and Affordable Care Act" is the polar opposite of what the practical outcome of this legislation will be. When this legislation is fully implemented the implications of the myriad of changes that it will bring will result in most citizens receiving a lower quality of health care and at an overall higher cost. There are two reasons for this. First, healthcare is being placed under the supervision and authority of the federal government. Centralized government is the most ineffective and inefficient method of executing any program, with the only exception being the waging of war. Second, Obamacare brings more citizens in to the healthcare system at once than ever before, which will result in the need for healthcare rationing, because there will be insufficient resources for the demand placed on the system as Obamacare is constructed. The argument behind Obamacare is that a large number of our citizens are without health insurance of any kind, so they have no access to proper health care. So let's start with that argument. It is true that approximately 50 million Americans (16.5% of the population) have no health insurance. Well, that means that 83.5% of Americans do have health insurance. Think about that. Our current system is working relatively well for the vast majority of our citizens. So the question is, why not develop a "safety- net" program specifically for the unfortunate few who do not have health insurance? Why would you abolish the system that is working relatively well for the majority (83.5%) of the people in order to create a system to benefit the unfortunate few (16.5%) who are currently left out?

If your home has a plumbing problem, it would not be wise, or efficient or practical to tear down the house and rebuild it, would it? No, you would call a plumber to come to your home and diagnose and repair the problem. If your car stopped running because your alternator failed, which then drained your battery, would you have your car towed away and disposed of and then go and buy a new car? No. Obviously that would be completely ridiculous. You would simply replace the alternator and the battery, and the car would work just fine. These are two simple and seemingly silly comparisons. However, these are essentially, and in a practical manner of speaking, what Obama is doing to the healthcare insurance system of the U.S. It will eliminate as we currently know it the private health insurance market for those who currently benefit from it. Then your only choice will be to fall in to the "public option" health insurance program, unless you have the means with which to privately finance your health care. Socialized healthcare is not an effective solution for the majority of our citizens, compared to the private system that we currently have. There are numerous examples of socialized medicine in western Europe and in Canada. The wealthy citizens from Canada who can afford it, regularly come to the U.S. for their healthcare, because the U.S. privatized free-market system is superior to the public healthcare available in their own country.

I am going to summarize some of the facts regarding the harm that the Obamacare system will do to the economy, as well as to your current health insurance benefits, when it is fully implemented. When the plan as it is currently written is fully implemented there will be a federal law that will require all companies with 50 or more employees to provide health insurance coverage for their full time employees. If a company chooses not to provide health insurance coverage to their employees, then the company will be assessed a fine for non-compliance. These fines will be onerous, and damaging to the financial health of these small companies, and are known to be set at a level that will be lower than the cost of the health insurance premiums.

This will cause three potential calamites for the American worker. The first potential calamity will involve the small companies that literally cannot afford to provide the insurance and that ultimately cannot afford to pay the newly assessed federal fine either. These small companies will either completely fail, meaning the loss of all workers jobs, or they will have to lay off some of their employees and further reduce operating costs in order to be able to pay the fines and to survive under the law, or to get below the 50 employee threshold. The second potential calamity will involve small companies that are financially strong enough to absorb the newly assessed fines without having to lay off any workers. The effect on these small companies, of the new federal fine for not providing healthcare insurance to their employees, will be a significant reduction in available working capital (liquidity; aka cash). As a result these companies will not have the working capital that they need in order to be able to expand and grow, which will have a debilitating effect on job growth. The company will not have the working capital to hire new workers for new projects, or to give their existing workers merit pay increases. In these first two calamities it is the American worker who pays the bitter cost for Obamacare. The third potential calamity is the scenario that most of us will experience. This will affect the companies that already provide health insurance to their employees. Some of these companies will find that the expense of paying the federal penalty for not providing their employee's with health insurance is lower than the cost of actually providing the health insurance benefits.

Some of these companies will choose to stop providing the health insurance in favor of the penalty. The employees of these companies will then be shoved in to the "public option" for their health insurance. If this is you, then on that day you will become dependent upon the government's version of health insurance and you will quickly find out just what socialized medicine is all about. Get ready for "managed care" at its nightmarish worst. You will find out that costs will be managed by limiting the availability of healthcare. Now, you may be saying, wow that sounds very synical. But how else do you think the federal government is going to actually decrease healthcare costs? These are consequences that are coming. This is legislation that has been passed by the Congress and signed in to law by the President. Unless it is repealed, this is going to happen.

I contend that the better alternative to this radical big government take-over of the entire nation's health care system is to repeal Obamacare and keep the free market private insurance system for the 83.5% of the population that it serves. (There are some changes and improvements needed for this imperfect system, but that is for another conversation.) Instead of

Obamacare, we need to develop a "safety-net" health insurance program

for the 16.5% of our citizens who cannot currently get existing health

insurance. This nation sent a man to the moon. I know we can figure this

out! If we are going to address the problem of the 16.5%uninsured

population, we need to understand who these people are and why they are

not insured.

A majority of employers (approximately 60%) offer group health insurance

policies to their employees and family members. Approximately 44% of the

U.S. population is covered by employer provided health insurance.

Employer provided health insurance is the largest source of health

insurance coverage in the nation under current circumstances. Prior to

Obamacare, employer sponsored health insurance was voluntary

(businesses were not legally required to offer a health benefit). Those who

do offer the benefit do so to be competitive and to attract skilled workers to

their business. Employees can refuse to participate, and some do because

they are covered by a spouse's insurance benefit. Some refuse coverage due to the employee share of the premium cost. The health of the economy is a critical factor for employer provided benefits. Recessionary and stagrant growth economies will harm employer's ability to provide health insurance benefits. This is illustrated by the fact that employer provided health insurance coverage was nearly 50% of the U.S. population in 2008, before the recession crippled the American economy.

Private policies purchased directly in the non-group market (outside of employer-sponsored benefits) covers only 5% of Americans. Private non-group health insurance premiums are more expensive than group coverage purchased by employers, with the cost varying by age and health status.

Government health insurance covers approximately 34% of the U.S. population (prior to Obamacare). There are several government health insurance programs covering specific qualifying participants. Medicare is the health insurance program that covers senior citizens beginning at age 65. Medicare also covers people who are under age 65 but who have a long term disability. The Medicare program currently covers approximately 47 million Americans (15% of the population). However, as the "baby boom" generation ages the Medicare program is projected to increase to as

many as 80 million participants by 2030. Medicaid is a health insurance

program primarily for low income individuals. The income threshold is very

low and the participants tend to be pregnant women, children and babies,

low income disabled people and low income elderly. The Medicaid

program currently covers approximately 63 million Americans (20% of the

population). Because Medicaid is primarily a low income program, it should

be considered to be a "safety-net" welfare program. Medicaid is a program

that is directly impacted by the health of the nation's economy. A

recessionary economy as well as a stagnant growth economy will drive

higher enrollments in Medicaid. The State Children's Health Insurance

Program (SCHIP) is a government health insurance program designed to

cover uninsured children in families with modest incomes that are too high

to qualify for Medicaid. This program is federally funded and administered

at the State level. SCHIP covers approximately 7 million children. The

remaining government health insurance programs primarily cover active military personnel, retired personnel, and their family members or surviving family members.

So from this background discussion of the existing insurance coverages that are currently available in the U.S., we see that already 35% of the nation's citizens are covered by government insurance. We are being told that health care costs are sky rocketing and that the health insurance system is not working. <u>So how is putting 100% of the citizens in to a government system going to be better, when the government can't manage the 35% that it has now?!! Think about that!</u>

Obamacare is a bad idea for several reasons: (1) it puts an industry that is characterized as suffering from rising costs, under the control of a federal government that cannot balance its own budget and is sinking rapidly in to catastrophic levels of debt; (2) if the federal government cannot effectively manage Medicare and Medicaid (35% of the market), what makes you think it can effectively manage the entire nation's health insurance?; (3) There WILL BE new and higher taxes as a result of Obamacare, at a time when the economy needs growth and investment incentive. Never raise taxes during a recession or in a stagnant growth economy! The effect on the economy will be negative. (4) Obamacare is the introduction of socialism to America. Socialism does not work. Western Europe's financial crisis is proof that socialism won't work long term. The free market economy works because the majority of the people are productive. In socialism, when a majority lives off of a productive minority, the economy will implode. (5) The Constitution is based upon freedom, liberty and limited government. Obamacare goes against every good Constitutional principal that created this country, developed this society and defines the American spirit of liberty and exceptionalism.

The Supreme Court made it clear in its opinion to uphold the legislation, that Obamacare is lawful only because the individual mandate is a tax under the Congress' taxing authority. Obama and his supporters from the beginning have denied that the healthcare legislation was a tax increase of any kind, because they wanted to hide this reality from you, the voter. Obama wants you to believe that this government healthcare plan is a benefit that will cost less than you are paying for your health insurance now. The Obama administration knows that is not true. And now you know it too. The Supreme Court opined that the new healthcare law could not be allowed under the "Commerce Clause" or the "Necessary and Proper Clause". These are the two relevant clauses in the Constitution that give Congress the power to act, and under these relevant clauses Obamacare was found to be unconstitutional with the individual mandate (forcing individuals to purchase health insurance). However, the court allowed Obamacare as a tax being assessed by Congress. The light of day has just been shown on Obama and his healthcare program. It is a massive tax increase that primarily the middle class of America will have to pay for. And it will cost you a lot more than you are paying for your health insurance currently. This is why it is so important for the well-being of our economy and our country, to FIRE OBAMA IN NOVEMBER and for Congress to repeal the healthcare legislation in the next legislative session!

In July 2012 after the Supreme Court Decision to uphold the healthcare legislation, The House of Representatives voted 244-185 to repeal Obamacare. This effort must be continued in the next session of Congress following Obama's defeat in November. This is legislation that the American public does not want, and that ultimately will degrade patient rights and individual healthcare choices. Obamacare's new regulations, taxes and mandates are hurting the already weak economy by crushing any incentive for job growth. It is a key reason that the unemployment rate (14% real unemployment) remains high. Voter dissatisfaction with the healthcare law was a major reason that Republicans took back control in the House of Representatives in the 2010 elections, and that voter dissatisfaction is a major reason why we will FIRE OBAMA IN NOVEMBER.

If nothing else that I have said here makes the case for how bad Obamacare will be, think about this anecdotal illustration. Have you noticed the many stories in the news, from time-to-time, regarding people who are mistreated and in some cases just completely abused or humiliated by TSA agents? There are a lot of news stories about these incidents, and it happens a lot more than what you actually see reported. So why does this happen? It is quite simple. Authority, with no competition for service and no fear of reprisal. Think about it. You have absolutely no choice, if you want to get on an airplane in the U.S., you have to submit yourself to the TSA agents and their procedures. You have no power to argue with them. You had better smile and comply or you will not be getting through security to board your flight! The TSA agents have no reason or motivation to be nice to you, or to provide any extra service to you or anyone else. They have a manual, and some procedures. If you don't comply, then you don't get through security. Period. Once Obamacare is fully implemented and all healthcare is under the government umbrella, and there are more people in the "system" than the system is capable of handling within reason…are you getting the picture? Do you really think that you will be treated any better by Obamacare than by the TSA. Government agencies are all the same. You will just be a number in the system. Please believe me here, you do not want to trust your health and well-being to a bloated, inefficient, over-loaded and likely incompetent government bureaucracy!

Obamacare is a deceptive attempt by the liberal Democrat party lead by a most ideological President, without any regard for the negative consequences for the country and the economy, to use healthcare to make the American citizens wholly dependent on the government for their well-being. It flies in the face of the liberty and freedom that define the birth and history of this great nation and its people. Obamacare is a disaster for the economy. We must stop the healthcare law, and repeal it, before it is fully implemented in 2014. We don't have much time. We must FIRE OBAMA IN NOVEMBER.

Chapter Five

Regulation and Taxation

The U.S unemployment rate has remained over 8%for an unprecedented three and a half years. That has not occurred since the end of World War II. Just in case you don't understand, that is a very bad thing for our economy. We have previously discussed that the real unemployment rate is actually over 14% when accounting for the under-employed and the qualified but dis-heartened job hunters who have given up on their job search. One of the biggest reasons for the lack of job growth in the American economy is the heavy handed and stifling regulations inflicted on the business and industry segments by the federal government. Much of the regulation goes well beyond what is needed to protect the citizens from "bad business practices". Much of the regulation is ideological in nature, and is aimed at targeted political themes and causes. The volume of new, business-killing regulatory actions by the Obama administration is beyond belief. We will discuss this critical issue in this chapter.

Following is an excerpt from a speech that President Obama gave in early July during a campaign appearance: "Look, if you've been successful, you didn't get there on your own. You didn't get there on your own! I'm always struck by people who think, well, it must be because I was just so smart. There are a lot of smart people out there. It must be because I worked harder than everybody else." "If you've got a business; you didn't build that. Somebody else made that happen. The internet didn't get invented on its own. Government research created the internet so that all the companies could make money off the internet." This is a chilling, arrogant, infuriating and very enlightening statement by the President. It tells you everything you need to know about his opinion of, and his attitude toward, the free market and entrepreneurism; the very foundations of the American economy. President Obama believes that the federal government is the foundation for business and economic growth. Therein lies the problem! He apparently did not study economics in his college curriculum, or if he did he didn't learn or retain much. President Obama said the private sector was "doing fine" in a campaign speech in June. The private sector has not been fine for over four years! But this is what this President believes, because he is an ideologue. He believes that American economic strength is derived not from private enterprise or individual exceptionalism, but from the collective, and ultimately, the government. If this wasn't so dangerous it would be laughable. But it is dangerous. This man has a chance at re-election, and if he wins re-election the American economy is "toast", and will not stand a chance at recovering from the recession that brought it to its knees in 2008.

Businesses do not hire employees because they are trying to be nice and help people out. Businesses hire employees to perform tasks and roles that help the business to earn money. To sell a product or a service. In the same manner you do not go to a store and spend money to be nice or to make sure that the employees have a job. You buy products and services that you need and/or that fill your wants and desires. That is reality.

For a business to plan to hire new employees, the business must see an opportunity and be willing to take a risk to gain new market share. To make more money! If a business detects more risk than opportunity, because of costly government regulations, or incrementally higher taxes and fees, then the business will likely look for a better environment in which to invest its capital and other resources. These are the basic facts that Obama completely ignores as he pursues his political aims first and foremost. And this is why for the first time since World War II the U.S. has sustained unemployment of over 8% for nearly four years. It is just that simple. This is why Obama MUST BE DEFEATED in NOVEMBER.

Some regulations are necessary and warranted to ensure the safety of the public as we use and consume products or services. For example, you want the construction standards for the containment facility of a nuclear power plant to be thorough and demanding, because the consequences of that product failure would be catastrophic. However, many regulations have been found to be unnecessary or excessive, and adding product cost beyond any reasonable measure of return on investment or public safety need. Every aspect of your daily life is affected, limited or controlled by the federal government's ever growing inventory of regulatory laws. Regulations control how we heat/cool our homes, how we light the rooms in our homes, the food that we buy and how we cook it, the toys that our children play with, the volume of television commercials, the gas can for your lawn mower and the toilet in your bathroom! All regulations add steps to the process of planning, testing, documenting and manufacturing the goods that are affected. These added steps add costs to these products, and those added costs are passed on to you the consumer.

Basic items such as toilets, showerheads, light bulbs, mattresses, washing machines, dryers, cars, ovens, refrigerators, television sets and bicycles all cost significantly more because of government intervention in the areas of energy use, product labeling and performance standards, in ways that go far beyond basic safety. The following regulations are extremely costly in terms of the added cost to the product which is born by the consumer: fuel economy and emission standards for passenger cars, light duty trucks, and medium duty passenger vehicles, as well as energy conservation standards for light bulbs. Many of these standards imposed by the government have become political in nature with respect to energy conservation. The costs of these regulations are oppressive and you pay the price every time you purchase one of these products. From entering office through 2011, the Obama administration has imposed 75 new regulations with reported costs to the private sector exceeding $40 billion. No other President has burdened businesses and individuals with a higher number or a larger cost of regulations in a comparable time period. Remember we talked in chapter three about the regulatory penalties that are being inflicted on the coal fueled power plants at the direction of Obama by the EPA. Those regulatory actions will add 10 to 20 percent to all electric bills in 2015 when the regulations are fully implemented. I am not even going in to the myriad of regulatory impacts and costs caused by the Dodd-Frank Finance bill. And then there is Obamacare (Patient Protection and Affordable Care Act).

Here is another cost of regulations that should hit close to home for you. When President Obama was inaugurated in January 2009 the price of gasoline was under $2.00 per gallon. During his term the price of gasoline has steadily climbed, reaching as high as $4.00 per gallon and as of this writing is hovering around $3.50 per gallon. That is nearly double the price of three years ago. It is not all Obama's fault that the price of gasoline has risen. But he is primarily to blame, because he is instituting industry regulations regarding oil exploration that is limiting the ability to explore and produce new sources of oil. He is also making bad policy decisions, including the Keystone XL pipeline that is further limiting the oil industry to import and refine oil from domestic and near domestic sources.

Once regulations are put on the books, then the regulatory agencies have to enforce these new rules. That costs a lot of money! The increasing regulations require a growing government workforce to regulate the industries. The regulatory staff for federal agencies grew three percent in 2009 and 2010, and grew by four percent in 2011. We did not have private sector job growth anywhere near those levels! The fatter the federal government gets the more expensive it is, and you pay for it! Barack Obama is using regulations as his trump card to get done what he is unable to achieve through the legislative process. It is a deceitful and underhanded strategy, used by an ideologue who does not have the best interests of the American citizens at heart.

Now we need to talk about tax policy. Tax policy is a key issue for two reasons. First, tax policy if used correctly (in conjunction with reasonable regulatory reform) can be THE strategy to re-ignite the economic engine of America, and generate REAL and long term job growth. This is really not debatable as it has been done successfully numerous times in American history. It is so simple. The second reason that tax policy is key, is that Democrats generally use "tax the rich" tax theory to fool uninformed voters in to believing that "someone else" can be compelled to pay their share because they have a higher income. Those of us who understand economic reality within the existing tax code, and can see what has happened repeatedly in history, know that "taxing the rich" by increasing marginal tax rates, does not work. It is a farce.

So here is the historically accurate reality of tax policy. Raising marginal tax rates ("tax the rich") will ultimately LOWER the amount of tax revenue collected by the IRS. Higher rates equal LOWER tax revenue! On the other hand decreasing marginal tax rates over a sustained period will increase the amount of tax revenue collected by the IRS. This is the opposite of what you will be told by the Democrats and the main stream media. Oh, and Obama too. I have found four historical examples of tax cuts working dramatically to grow the economy, and accelerate job growth as well as to help the government by increasing the amount of tax revenue paid in to the U.S. Treasury!

The first example is from the 1920s. In the 20s U.S. Treasury Secretary Andrew Mellon pointed out that people with high incomes were not paying the high tax rates, because they were putting their money in to legal tax shelters. He argued that if the government would cut the marginal tax rate on the high income earners, that investments would flow back into the private sector which would cause the overall economy to grow , increasing individual tax payer incomes, creating new jobs and ultimately as a result would increase the total federal tax revenue. So, in the mid-1920s the federal government cut the corporate income tax rate first, and then cut the individual marginal rates across the board. The highest tax bracket was cut from 73% down to 25%. The tax cuts allowed the U.S. economy to grow rapidly during the mid and late 1920s. In 1924 the total annual federal tax revenue was $704 million, but after the marginal tax rates were reduced, at the end of 1928 the total annual federal tax revenue had increased to $1.164 billion, a growth of 65% in just four years. Higher total tax revenue from lower marginal tax rates! Here is the really interesting statistical breakdown: (1) the highest income earner tax bracket paid a higher share of the total individual income taxes, increasing from $300 million in 1924 (43%) to $700 million in 1928 (61%); (2) between 1924 and 1928 the number of individual tax payers earning less than $10,000 per year declined, while the number of tax payers earning between $10,000 and $100,000 per year increased by 84 percent! So as the high earners invested and created jobs, those who needed the new jobs had their earnings and lifestyles improved. Tax cuts for the rich indeed! Between 1924 and 1929, real gross national product grew at an annual average rate of 4.7 percent and the unemployment rate fell from 6.7 percent to 3.2 percent. The Mellon tax cuts restored incentives to work, save, and invest and discouraged the use of tax shelters. All tax payers benefitted and the federal government received more federal tax revenue.

The second example of cutting marginal tax rates and stimulating the

economy took place in the 1960s. This chart will illustrate the discussion:

			United States Federal Tax Revenues				
			(millions of dollars)				
Year	Individual income tax		Corporate income tax		Soc Sec & other taxes	Total tax revenue	
1960	40,715		21,494		30,282	92,491	
1961	41,338	1.5%	20,954	-2.5%	32,095	94,387	2.0%
1962	45,571	10.2%	20,523	-2.1%	33,581	99,675	5.6%
1963	47,588	4.4%	21,579	5.1%	37,393	106,560	6.9%
1964	48,697	2.3%	23,493	8.9%	40,425	112,615	5.7%
1965	48,792	0.2%	25,461	8.4%	42,565	116,818	3.7%
1966	55,446	13.6%	30,073	18.1%	45,316	130,835	12.0%
1967	61,526	11.0%	33,971	13.0%	53,325	148,822	13.7%
1968	68,726	11.7%	28,665	-15.6%	55,582	152,973	2.8%
1969	87,249	27.0%	36,678	28.0%	62,955	186,883	22.2%

Source: Office of Management and Budget

The Presidential election in 1960 took place in a stagnating economy.

Growth in the gross national product during the 1950s had averaged about

2.4 percent per year, which is a relatively slow rate of growth. Then there

was an actual recession in 1960 during the campaign. The Democrat

candidate John F. Kennedy, stressed the need for economic growth. The

newly elected Kennedy administration proposed federal spending initiatives

as an economic stimulus program, however the Congress would not pass the legislation for the proposed reduced spending programs (sounds like the current Congress). So President Kennedy resorted to a proposal for tax cuts. In 1962 the Kennedy administration restructured the depreciation allowance, which provided capital investment incentives to small businesses and corporate America. The corporate income tax rate was cut from 52% to 48%. Individual income tax rates were also cut moderately, with the top tax rate reduced from 90 percent to 70 percent, and the lowest marginal rate cut from 20 percent to 14 percent. Would you like to guess what happened? You can refer to the eye chart on the prior page for the hard numbers. From 1962 to 1969 the tax revenue from individual tax payers increased from $45.6 billion to $87.2 billion, a growth rate of 91.5% over eight years! The tax revenue from corporations increased from $20.5 billion to $36.7 billion, a growth rate of 79% in eight years! The growing federal tax revenue was the result of an expansion of the economy which also included growth in the jobs market. The unemployment rate was 5.5% in 1960, which compared to today is very low. However, the unemployment rate dropped to 3.8% in 1966, and was at 3.5% in 1969, prior to the repeal of the Kennedy tax cuts that occurred in 1970.

Another example of cutting marginal tax rates and stimulating the economy took place in the 1980s.

United States Federal Tax Revenues
(millions of dollars)

Year	Individual income tax		Corporate income tax		Soc Sec & other taxes	Total tax revenue	
1980	244,069		64,600		208,443	517,112	
1981	285,917	17.1%	61,137	-5.4%	252,218	599,272	15.9%
1982	297,744	4.1%	49,207	-19.5%	270,815	617,766	3.1%
1983	288,938	-3.0%	37,022	-24.8%	274,603	600,563	-2.8%
1984	298,415	3.3%	56,893	53.7%	311,129	666,438	11.0%
1985	334,531	12.1%	61,331	7.8%	338,175	734,037	10.1%
1986	348,959	4.3%	63,143	3.0%	357,053	769,155	4.8%
1987	392,557	12.5%	83,926	32.9%	377,804	854,287	11.1%
1988	401,181	2.2%	94,508	12.6%	413,549	909,238	6.4%
1989	445,690	11.1%	103,291	9.3%	442,123	991,104	9.0%

Source: Office of Management and Budget

From 1977-1980 Jimmy Carter was the President, and he was arguably the most inept President in modern history. In November 1980 Carter ran for re-election against Ronald Reagan. Reagan won in a landslide taking 51% of the popular vote, winning 44 states and 91% of the electoral votes! President-elect Reagan inherited an economic mess including: 7.5%

unemployment, 12.5% inflation and 18% prime lending rate. Can you

imagine having an 18% mortgage interest rate? President Reagan's first

major legislation was the Economic Recovery Tax Act of 1981. This

legislation cut individual tax rates across the board over a three year period

by 23%. The top individual rate was reduced from 70% to 50% and the

lowest rate was cut from 14% to 11%. This tax legislation also indexed the

tax code for inflation to prevent "tax bracket creep" that was very prevalent

in the 1970s because of the high inflation rate. Businesses were given

investment incentive due to the allowance of accelerated depreciation

deductions, which encouraged investment in depreciable (big and

expensive) business equipment and infrastructure.

The results from these changes in tax policy were astounding. From 1980

to 1988, inflation dropped from 13.5% to 4.1%, unemployment declined

from 7.6% to 5.5%, real gross national product increased by 26%, and

there were 20 million new jobs created! How does 2 million new jobs per

year sound to you right now?! The total annual federal tax revenue nearly

doubled during President Reagan's two terms (see the chart on the previous page – Total Tax Revenue), from $517 billion the year before he was elected to nearly $1 trillion at the end of his second term. For my friends on the left who still think tax cuts are "for the rich", in 1981 before the tax rate reductions, the top 10% of wage earners paid 48% of the total tax revenue. In 1988 the top 10% of wage earners were paying 57% of all federal tax revenue. Cutting the marginal rates resulted in more total tax revenue being collected, and resulted in an even higher percentage of tax being paid by the highest wage earners. And it fueled huge economic growth. Those who dispute these facts are either completely dishonest, or they are ideologically blinded. And for the record, Ronald Reagan was a great President! He revived the U.S. economy and he brought down the iron curtair. His decisions and his policies were in the best interests of this country and its citizens, not based on some crazed ideology from the back halls of liberal institutions. We need another Ronald Reagan!

The fourth and the most recent example, of reducing marginal tax rates and stimulating the economy took place in 2003 under George W. Bush ("W" as I like to refer to him). If Ronald Reagan was one of the most beloved

Presidents of the modern era, George W. Bush may be one of the most hated Presidents, by his detractors, for several reasons. Personally I loved "W" because he responded decisively to the terrorist attacks of 9/11/2001 and he kept the country safe through his actions for the rest of his Presidency. There are those who not only disagreed with W, as they are entitled to, but there was a vehement hate for him that was loudly proclaimed publicly. It was partly due to the election of 2000 when the US Supreme Court had to make a decision regarding the Florida electoral votes. When the Supreme Court decided in favor of W, it gave him the margin of victory and he won the election over Al Gore. So the beginning of his Presidency was controversial to say the least. Then there was the controversy over the Iraq war. That was an issue of deep emotion for many people. So, with W most people either loved him or hated him. But, I digress...

The Bush Administration proposed legislation initially in 2001 and then finalized in 2003, known as the Jobs and Growth Tax Relief Reconciliation Act of 2003. The primary purpose of this legislation was to provide tax relief and investment incentive to businesses and individuals in an effort to stimulate the economy. (stimulating the economy is one of the top jobs of every President!) W's tax policy basically had three major components: (1) it increased the rate of depreciation allowed and also increased the allowance for an expense election in lieu of depreciation (i.e. expense the full amount of a $5,000 computer in the year it is purchased, rather than depreciating it over 5 years); (2) decreased the capital gains tax rates from 10% and 20%, to 5% and 15%(that may not sound like much, but the stimulative effect is significant); and (3) cut individual tax rates: the top rate declined from 39% to 35%, the middle rate declined from 31% to 28% and the lower rate declined from 28% to 25%. The lowest rates were unchanged.

United States Federal Tax Revenues
(millions of dollars)

Year	Individual income tax		Corporate income tax		Soc Sec & other taxes	Total tax revenue	
2000	1,004,462		207,289		813,447	2,025,198	
2001	994,339	-1.0%	151,075	-27.1%	845,728	1,991,142	-1.7%
2002	858,345	-13.7%	148,044	-2.0%	846,760	1,853,149	-6.9%
2003	793,699	-7.5%	131,778	-11.0%	856,844	1,782,321	-3.8%
2004	808,959	1.9%	189,371	43.7%	881,796	1,880,126	5.5%
2005	927,222	14.6%	278,282	47.0%	948,121	2,153,626	14.5%
2006	1,043,908	12.6%	353,915	27.2%	1,009,053	2,406,876	11.8%
2007	1,163,472	11.5%	370,243	4.6%	1,034,286	2,568,001	6.7%
2008	1,145,747	-1.5%	304,346	-17.8%	1,073,898	2,523,991	-1.7%
2009	915,308	-20.1%	138,229	-54.6%	1,051,452	2,104,988	-16.6%

Source: Office of Management and Budget

The results from these tax incentives were relatively good. Refer to the chart above for the following: (1) individual federal income tax revenue to the Treasury stabilized in 2004 after three consecutive years of declines, and then had three consecutive years of double digit growth; (2) U.S. corporations income tax paid to the Treasury more than doubled from 2004 to 2007; (3) overall the total federal tax revenue grew by 24.6% during W's two terms in office!

OK. So I have laid out four specific examples of the use of marginal tax rate reductions as an effective stimulus of the U.S. economy which resulted in the growth of the economy (GDP), the growth in economically viable jobs and as a result an increase in the amount of federal tax revenue collected by the U.S. Treasury. These four examples occurred in four completely unrelated points in time, literally separated by decades. So the facts show that this is an effective way to stimulate the economy and create job growth.

In looking at the charts that I have provided in this chapter you may have noticed that individuals pay the majority of the taxes in the United States. That is the nature of our economy. The individual consumer is the engine that drives the U.S. economy. That is why job growth stability is so critical to the well-being of the U.S. economy. Another important factor that I pointed out earlier in the chapter is that the highest wage earners in the U.S. pay the majority of the income taxes. So when you hear "tax cuts for the rich", remember that the "rich" as they are so affectionately called, are paying now, and have always paid throughout history, more than their "fair share"!

I want to briefly touch on a subject that is pure politics. To this point I have tried to stick to the facts as I have supported my opinions. But now I need to get political, because this is used by your elected leaders and by the press in very effective ways, to shape your opinion. When the subject of tax cuts are discussed, sooner or later our friends on the left are going to say that tax cuts are the reason for the budget deficits. In other words they are saying that tax cuts cause the budget deficits because tax cuts will cause lower tax revenues. However, now with the history lessons that I have given you from the 20s, the 60s, the 80s and with W since 2000, you now know that this assertion is factually untrue! <u>The truth is that we have budget deficits because the Congress is spending more money than the Treasury is collecting!</u> It is just that simple. Our elected leaders have been irresponsible in the financial management of our government. If you ran your household the way that Congress has been running our country, you would be bankrupt! When corporate CEOs run their companies irresponsibly either the company fails, or the CEO gets fired and the company changes its financial practices in order to survive. This is exactly where the United States government stands today. Our CEO (the President) is an irresponsible leader and he needs to be fired, so that we can change the direction that our government is taking our country and our economy. We cannot wait until later to deal with this. We cannot hope that someone else will handle this for us. We must do the things necessary to change how our government is run NOW. The first thing to do is FIRE OBAMA in November!

The "Bush tax cuts" had a sunset, meaning they only lasted until December 31, 2010. At that time the tax rates were scheduled to go back up to the previous higher levels. President Obama extended the Bush tax cuts for two years, through December 31, 2012. Why would he do that? Well it is very simple. President Obama knew that if he allowed the tax rates to go back up, while the economy was in the midst of a recession, or in the early stage of a recovery, the economy would fall back in to the recession due to the negative effects of the tax increases. President Obama knew that the timing of that would be very bad for his re-election in 2012. I will assure you that President Obama will tell you that he intends to ask Congress to extend the sunset of the tax cuts again at December 31, 2012. However, if he gets re-elected in November, he never has to worry about another election. So there is no way he will extend the tax cuts. That goes against his ideology. He will raise taxes just the same way that he has increased numerous government regulations to institute policy to further his liberal and environmental priorities. The tax increases will devastate the economy. The tax increases are so substantial that they are already being discussed in news stories, and have been named "Taxmageddon". I cannot emphasize enough, just how devastating an effect these tax increases will have on the economy if it is allowed to happen. Don't take a chance with your future. Don't allow Obama the chance to let the Bush tax cuts expire. FIRE OBAMA in November.

I would like to end this chapter with a funny little riddle from my hero, and one of our greatest Presidents, Ronald Reagan. You may remember this from his campaign against Jimmy Carter. My version goes like this: a Recession is when your neighbor loses his job; a Depression is when you lose your job; a Recovery is when Barack Obama loses his job! It is time

for a real recovery in America, so let's make it happen in November!

Chapter 6

Obama has to go!

On the last page of chapter one I said that I would give you five reasons why re-electing Barack Obama will greatly harm our country and reduce the standard of living for American citizens. Chapters two through five covered those five reasons in detail. I will recap the five reasons so that you have an abbreviated list to remember, and to share with anyone that you discuss or debate these issues with:

1. Unsustainable debt – The Obama administration has increased the national debt by $4.8 trillion in 3 years; more than any other President in history; the U.S. credit rating has been down-graded for the first time in history as a result. Obama has no plan to reduce spending, no goal to balance the budget, and indicates no serious intention of dealing with the precipitously growing debt. Totally irresponsible!

2. Bad Energy Policy – The Obama administration has wasted nearly $100 billion of tax payer money on the Green Energy folly. Government should encourage free market development through tax incentives, not by literally

giving money away. Obama's energy policies have contributed to rising gasoline prices (under $2/gallon on 1/1/2009; now nearly $4/gallon), imposed oppressive regulations on the energy industry, and will unnecessarily lead to significantly higher electricity prices by 2015. Again, there is no indication of concern for the citizen's pain from rising energy costs. He is pursuing his agenda, and America be damned. Totally irresponsible!

3. Healthcare – Socialism - The Obama healthcare program will federalize the entire healthcare system; the same government which cannot balance its budget and is precipitously running up unsustainable debt wants you to trust your health and well-being to its management oversight; do you really want to have to trust the government to take care of your healthcare, with their TSA style attitude, procedures and behavior? I know that I sure don't!! The government option is always more expensive and less efficient than private options. Always! Another example of Obama pursuing his ideological agenda, and not trying to better the country. Totally irresponsible.

4. Regulations – The hidden tax. Regulations add costs to the products that they are assessed on, and those additional costs are passed on to the consumer. Regulations burden businesses and stifle job growth. President Obama has used oppressive regulations to accomplish the policy objectives that he was unable to accomplish through legislation (Congress). With his "if you've got a business, you didn't build that" comment in July, President Obama made it clear that he thinks government is the answer. Regulations are another blatant example of Obama pursuing his ideological agenda, and ignoring the costs and consequences that the American people bear now, and even more in the future.

5. Taxmageddon – The economy killer. If re-elected, Obama will allow the Bush tax cuts to expire, which will unleash a massive tax increase on America on January 1, 2013. In addition, there are numerous tax increases embedded in Obamacare that will begin to be assessed as the program is implemented beginning in 2014. The tax increases will kill any chance for recovery or growth in the economy. This economy is still very weak, with

anemic (less than inflation) GDP growth and punishing unemployment levels (real unemployment is 14%!).

This is not a matter of race or religion or any personal characteristic. This is about bad policy and the terrible consequences that Obama's bad policy agenda is inflicting upon the American economy and upon you, the American citizens. If you have children or grandchildren, or if you plan to live a long and productive life, you must vote to remove Obama from office in November. There is no question now about what he is about, or what he plans to do. We have nearly 4 years of performance and policy and legislation and regulations. In 2008 we heard about "hope and change". Now I am just hoping for A CHANGE, in the White House!

On a personal note, for me another reason for firing Obama with this election is the fact that he chose Joe Biden as his Vice President. Amongst his friends and family, Joe Biden may be a real nice man. I don't know him personally. But as a public figure, when I hear him speaking to the country as the Vice President, I see him as an arrogant, condescending buffoon! A person's true character comes out when they are placed in a position of power. Maybe Obama picked Biden as his VP just to show us that he doesn't really need one. Whatever the case, I don't want to see Joe Biden glaring down his nose at me, and lecturing me while wagging that finger at me. Remember his "don't screw with me" confrontation with the little reporter? If not, internet-search it. His behavior is beneath the dignity that I expect from the Vice President of the United State of America.

I have spent this entire book documenting for you why you should not vote to re-elect Barack Obama. So you may be wondering, what do I expect you to do in the alternative? That is very simple. You go to your polling place on election day and you vote for Mitt Romney. Mr. Romney is a good man of high character. His personal accomplishments in his life and career are astounding. He is intelligent and well spoken. He has the stature and the dignity to be a President that you can be proud of, and confident in, to represent us in the way that taking the oath of office demands.

You can go to mittromney.com and read all of his policy statements for yourself. But I will give you a brief summary from my reading of his site and from listening to him campaign. On "run-away" federal spending:

Romney wants to cap federal non-defense spending. This is a good move. It will make the government manage and prioritize programs the same way that you and I have to manage our personal spending: do what is most important with what you have. It won't balance the budget immediately, as that would be economically unlikely and also would be unwise as it would have a negative effect on the economic recovery. It will stop the rapid growth of spending and will narrow the annual budget deficit. It is a strategy that gets us going in the right direction. I agree with this approach.

On taxes: Romney believes that lowering individual marginal tax rates will incentivize economic growth and ultimately will result in higher tax revenue due to growth of the economy. Hallelujah brother! I have a chapter in this book to prove that this is sound policy. I heartily agree with this approach. He also has some ideas for simplifying the tax code. I think that is a good idea, but it will take some time. Romney believes that we should cut the corporate ncome tax rate. Atta boy! Again a very wise move that will result in economic growth domestically, and will bring more capital in to the

U.S. for investment and job growth. This is very sound policy, and I definitely support this.

On Energy: Romney wants to encourage and incentivize domestic production of energy resources, while managing environmental impacts in sensitive areas. This is very wise! We need to produce as much of our own energy as possible. That reduces energy costs and creates and sustains American job growth. I agree with Mitt. Romney also disagrees with Obama on the Keystone XL pipeline. We covered this topic in chapter three. Obama was wrong to block the Keystone XL pipeline. Stop the absolute foolish regulation of carbon dioxide (CO_2). Romney wants to encourage research and development for all energy resources, including alternative sources. Alternative energy funding will be continued, but through basic research. Basically he wants to have the government get out of the way and let the American energy industry fuel the engine of democracy, while still considering future energy development. This is good policy.

On Healthcare: Romney says that when elected he will issue an executive order on day one that paves the way for the federal government to issue Obamacare waivers to all fifty states. He will then work with Congress to repeal the Obamacare legislation as soon as possible. In place of Obamacare he will pursue a policy returning the states to the proper place in charge of regulating local insurance markets and caring for the poor, uninsured, and chronically ill. He will ensure flexibility to help the uninsured by public-private partnerships, exchanges and subsidies. Empower individuals and small businesses to form purchasing pools. Prevent discrimination against individuals with pre-existing conditions. End tax discrimination against the individual purchase of insurance. Allow consumers to purchase insurance across state lines. These are sound free market objectives toward improving the healthcare coverage options to all citizens, without the oppressive taxation and regulation of Obamacare.

The election in November 2012 is not about Mitt Romney. This election is about the future of the United States of America. We know from the data that I have presented herein that the policies of Barack Obama have done great harm to the economy of the United States, evidenced by: the unprecedented and pro-longed high unemployment rate, the precipitously growing and unsustainable national debt, the embarrassment of the lowering of the U.S. credit rating, the unmitigated rising energy prices, and the socialistic, inefficient and individual unfriendly government healthcare program that will further inflate taxation, fees and the national debt. So while this election is not about Mitt Romney, it is about voting for Mitt Romney because he has the policy platform to correct the harmful actions of the Obama administration.

I will not stop my efforts to improve the outlook for our country with this little book. I have two children that I love and adore, and whom I want to see have productive, happy and successful lives. I want them to have the American opportunity for success that can be attained through hard work, when the government is not interfering in its citizens lives. I want to have a long and prosperous life unencumbered by a centralized impersonal federal government bureaucracy. And I want all of my fellow Americans to have these same benefits of living in the greatest country on the face of the earth!

So I will follow up this little book with further research and work and writing, to communicate to you my fellow Americans, the changes that are needed in all levels of our government to assure your God given liberties and your Constitutional rights and privileges. I will hold all public officials responsible for their behavior and actions. I will watch what "President Romney" does to insure that he follows through with his campaign commitments, and I will monitor the Congress and its members for their performance as well. There is much room for improvement in the Congress.

I thank God for the privilege of living in this, the greatest country in the world. There is no reason, aside from our own irresponsibility (demonstrated by the Obama administration policies), that the United States should not to be the leader of the world in economic viability, freedom and justice. It is our responsibility to be active in selecting our elected leaders, and to hold them responsible for their actions, or the lack thereof. Do not assume that everyone who is elected to serve in Washington DC will do so as promised in their campaign. We have to stay engaged with the important issues and what is being done about these issues.

Thank you for reading my book. God bless you, and God bless America! Now go vote for Mitt Romney on Tuesday November 6, 2012!

www.ingramcontent.com/pod-product-compliance
Lightning Source LLC
Chambersburg PA
CBHW022026170526
45157CB00003B/1374